Patricia Bath
and Laser Surgery

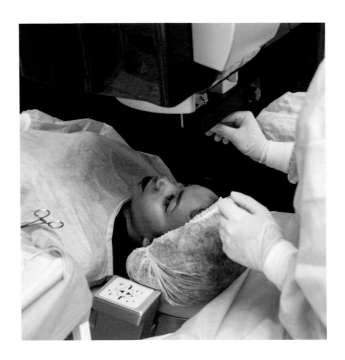

By Ellen Labrecque

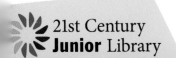
21st Century
Junior Library

Published in the United States of America by
Cherry Lake Publishing
Ann Arbor, Michigan
www.cherrylakepublishing.com

Content Adviser: Amelia Wenk Gotwals, Ph.D., Associate Professor of Science Education, Michigan State University
Reading Adviser: Marla Conn MS, Ed., Literacy specialist, Read-Ability, Inc.

Photo Credits: © Romaset/Shutterstock Images, cover; © AMR Image/iStock, 4; © Jemal Countess/Stringer/Getty Images, 6; © Everett Historical/Shutterstock Images, 8; © Webspark/Shutterstock Images, 10; © Joseph Sohm/Shutterstock Images, 12; © ARZTSAMUI/Shutterstock Images, 14; © Patricia E. Bath (US4744360)/United States Patent and Trademark Office, 16; © epa european pressphoto agency b.v. /Alamy Stock Photo, 18; © Abd. Halim Hadi/Shutterstock Images, 20

Library of Congress Cataloging-in-Publication Data
Names: Labrecque, Ellen, author.
Title: Patricia Bath and laser surgery / by Ellen Labrecque.
Description: Ann Arbor, MI : Cherry Lake Publishing, [2017] | Series: 21st century junior library. Women innovators | Audience: K to
    grade 3. | Includes bibliographical references and index.
Identifiers: LCCN 2016030055| ISBN 9781634721806 (hardcover) | ISBN 9781634723121 (pbk.) | ISBN 9781634722469 (pdf) |
    ISBN 9781634723787 (ebook)
Subjects: LCSH: Bath, Patricia, 1942–Juvenile literature. | Ophthalmologists–Biography–Juvenile literature. |
    Women inventors–Biography–Juvenile literature. | Eye–Surgery–Juvenile literature. | Lasers in surgery–History–
    Juvenile literature.
Classification: LCC RE36.B2855 L33 2017 | DDC 617.7092 [B]–dc23
LC record available at https://lccn.loc.gov/2016030055

Cherry Lake Publishing would like to acknowledge the work of The Partnership for 21st Century Skills.
Please visit *www.p21.org* for more information.

Printed in the United States of America
Corporate Graphics

CONTENTS

It is important to have your eyes examined regularly.

A Woman

Imagine if the world looked fuzzy. Or you couldn't see *anything* at all. You would want to visit a doctor. You would want to find out if you could do something to improve your vision.

Thanks to Patricia Bath, more people around the world have access to eye care. This includes eye exams, eyeglasses, and a very important surgery that Bath invented. Her **invention** helps people see!

As a woman and an African American, Bath had to overcome **sexism** and **racism** to achieve her goals.

Patricia Bath was born on November 4, 1942, in Harlem, New York. Her dad worked for the New York City Subway. He was also a newspaper writer. Her mom was a homemaker and housekeeper. Her parents thought school was important. Patricia studied hard and got good grades.

When Patricia was growing up, most girls were not encouraged to study math and science.

Patricia was especially smart in math and science. Her mother gave her a **chemistry kit** when she was young. She loved playing with it. She also loved to read. She graduated from high school in just two years. (Most students graduate from high school in four years.)

Create!

Pretend you could create a new magic potion using a chemistry set. What would you invent? Would you invent a liquid that made you invisible? How about one that could make you fly?

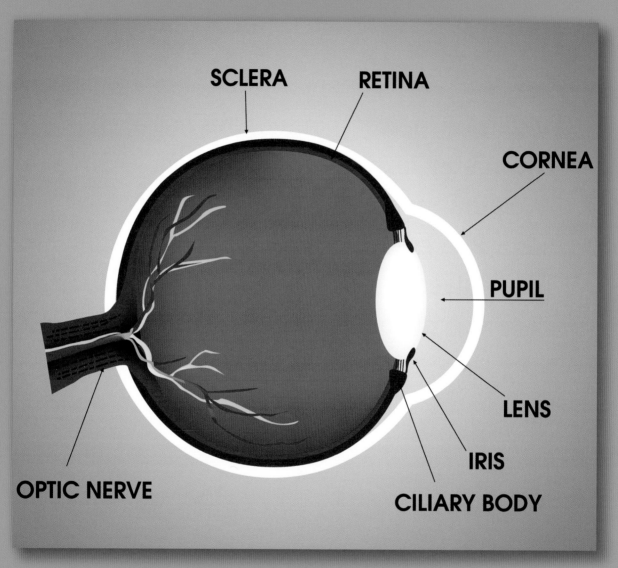

The brain is the only human organ more complex than the eye.

Bath went to medical school. Then, she studied **ophthalmology**. She wanted to become an eye doctor.

Bath noticed that poor African Americans had more eye problems than other people. They did not have good access to eye care. Their eye problems went untreated. They were more likely to go **blind**.

Look!

Look at this drawing of an eyeball. Study the parts of the eye. How do you think these parts help you see? Try to find more information about the eye on the Internet.

Bath wanted to make sure everyone had access to eye care.

An Idea

Bath created a new field of medicine called **community ophthalmology**. In this field, volunteers provide basic eye exams to poor communities. They help people get glasses, test for diseases, and prevent blindness. Bath also started a group called the American Institute for the Prevention of Blindness. She wanted to help people around the world see.

Cataracts are spots on people's eyes that make it hard for them to see.

In 1988, Bath invented the Laserphaco Probe. It is a device that is inserted into a tiny cut in the eye. Doctors can remove **cataracts** quickly and easily using this tool. Cataracts are spots that form on people's eyes as they age. They make vision cloudy.

Ask Questions!

Ask your grandma or grandpa if they have ever had cataract surgery. After the surgery, were they able to see more clearly?

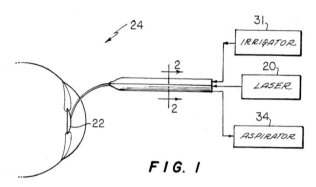

FIG. 1

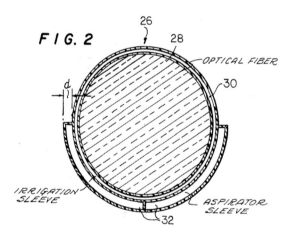

FIG. 2

To get her patent, Bath made detailed
drawings of her invention.

Once the cataract is removed, a new **lens** is inserted. Using Bath's device, doctors can help patients see clearly again! Bath is the first African American female doctor granted a **patent** for a medical invention.

Bath wants to make sure that as many people
as possible can see and enjoy the world!

A Legacy

Bath still does work around the world helping people see. She travels to poor countries. She does surgery on people for free. She went to North Africa. She helped a woman who had been blind for 30 years get her vision back! "The ability to restore sight is the ultimate award," she says.

Providing those in need with access to eye care is a worldwide challenge.

More than 40 million people worldwide are blind. Half of these people would be able to see if they had the right eye care. Bath's **legacy** is her desire to help these people through innovations like community ophthalmology and the Laserphaco Probe. She thinks everybody deserves the right to sight!

GLOSSARY

blind (BLINDE) unable to see

cataracts (KAT-uh-rakts) cloudy spots covering parts of the eye

chemistry kit (KEM-uh-stree KIT) a toy kids can use for the scientific study of substances, what they are composed of, and how they react with each other

community ophthalmology (kuh-MYOO-ni-tee of-thuhl-MOL-uh-jee) a field of medicine that involves volunteers providing basic eye exams in poor communities

invention (in-VEN-shun) something new created from imagination

legacy (LEG-uh-see) something handed down from one generation to another

lens (LENZ) the clear part of the eye that focuses light on the retina

ophthalmology (of-thuhl-MOL-uh-jee) the study of medicine dealing with the eye

patent (PAT-uhnt) the right granted by the government to use or sell an invention for a certain number of years

racism (RAY-sih-zum) treating people unfairly based on their race

sexism (SEK-sih-zum) treating people unfairly based on whether they are male or female

FIND OUT MORE

BOOKS

Henderson, Susan. *African-American Inventors III: Patricia Bath, Philip Emeagwali, Henry Sampson, Valerie Thomas, Peter Tolliver.* Mankato, MN: Capstone Press, 1998.

Hudson, Wade. *Book of Black Heroes: Scientists, Healers, and Inventors.* East Orange, NJ: Just Us Books, 2003.

Warren, Wini. *Black Woman Scientists in the United States.* Bloomington: Indiana University Press, 1999.

WEB SITES

Famous Black Inventors
www.black-inventor.com
Learn about other famous African American inventors.

Scholastic—Culture & Change: Black History in America
http://teacher.scholastic.com/activities/bhistory/inventors
Meet 14 scientists and inventors who changed history.

INDEX

ABOUT THE AUTHOR

Ellen Labrecque is a freelance writer living in Yardley, Pennsylvania. Previously, she was a senior editor at Sports Illustrated Kids. Ellen loves to travel and then learn about new places and people that she can write about in her books.